Words Versus Meanings
Selected Poems and Short Stories

Kevin A. Murphy

For Donny

ACKNOWLEDGMENTS

Thank you to all who have helped make this book possible, especially my family. To my loving parents, Larry and Lisa, who never gave up on me when I was down, and supported my creativity all along. To my younger sister, Molly, for the late-night conversations that bleed into morning, and for always expecting the best out of me—even when it meant shutting me out— you helped me survive. To my older sister, Abby, for having pride in me, always providing laughter, and giving me cookies.

Cover photography by Jacob McEachern: www.jacobjohnphotography.com, Facebook: Jacob J-Photography, Instagram: @jacobjphotography.

Author photo by Sam Smetana.

Cover design, interior design, and editing by Kevin A. Murphy.

Arrangement of Text

This book is divided into two sections: poems and short stories. The beginning of each section is introduced by a cover page.

Poems are introduced by the date they were written, and title when applicable. Poems longer than one page continue on subsequent pages; no page shares separate poems. Haikus are centered.

Short stories are introduced by title.

Poems

Words Versus Meanings
2.1.14

My words were daggers,
and in my murky,
whiskey-induced stupor,
I aimed them to pierce your spirit.
I don't recall the words themselves,
but their meanings reeked of loathing—
much like the scent of the T-shirt
clinging to my back.
I cannot tell whether my expressions reached you
in the midnight blue—that night—
through the dusk and the gloom,
but they were intended to.
I imagine this to be why I am so confused:
because I meant to say, "you're breathtaking."
If I were to ever enjoy
your presence again,
I envision that I might find you
lounging amongst the needle points of light
shining through the dark,
satin curtains of the nighttime heavens,
glowing
so much brighter than the rest.

7.14.15

You must be a magician
because these ribs are a cage
held shut by lock and key,
and yet,
you've stolen my heart.

5.27.15

voice cracked
like a whip
in midnight
air
your head rests
like a sun
set on my pillow
my fingers run
like rivers
through your hair
our feet inter
twined
under blankets
the recesses of my
mind
adrift in your
stare

7.18.13

Do you like butterflies?
Because a million
fly inside my stomach
every time you speak.
You can have a few
if you think they're beautiful;
I have all the beauty
I'll ever need in you.

8.12.16

I am;
I am a son, a survivor, a brother, a fighter,
a lover, a writer, a boy who grew into a
man, a ponderer, a wanderer, a shoulder
to cry on, and a passionate soul
with a plan.

For all the times
when identity comes into question,
I remind myself of the simple fact—
I am.

6.8.15

Time is relative—
you can save your theories—
I see this
when I look into her eyes
and it all stands still.

2.20.15

It's unreal
how real
you appear
when I sleep.

2.22.14

I'm beginning to understand
that being truthful
is not always synonymous
with being ethical.
I'm troubled to wonder
if I should thus expect
to live in a reality
somewhat written in lies.

In No Sense: A Dream
7.30.14

We ran in isolated
moments of delirium
and back alleys outside
of hotels in Las Vegas
or elsewhere.
We stomped and danced,
and sang
in puddles of rainwater,
and our clothes, and
our shoes,
and fuck our socks
got wet,
but we ceased to really care
about anything
like the tween-tech-kids of the
new millennium
who
rave to the new-age electronic
sounds of tomorrow
wearing checkered prints and neons,
and
not really having any idea
what in god's Name
they'll do tomorrow.
It was grand!
Before wayfarer-wearing nine-to-five hipsters
were glad they didn't wear checkers
and neon.
It was a place
in time,
but
the best part was
that it was an isolated moment
of delirium—

maybe somewhere near Seattle.
We boated into lakes of romantic naivety—
blue,
and orange,
and pink.
Maybe your black dress
accentuated the glass-like colors
and reflections of the lake,
or the green gum
you'd leave on the roof of my car
sometime around a year later
when the leaves began to fall—
orange—
on the roofs of the cars
and the houses
of the people in the area.
Maybe we only ever made it there by chance.
Galash! Galash!
We'd stomp in the rain,
sing songs we half-way remembered,
build fires,
swim,
and tell stories—stories
that provoked laughter in all of us.
Galash!
The rain!
Let's dance.
We'd dance, and swim,
and dance, and build fires,
and swim.
We'd laugh.
We'd drive to tomorrow
wherever tomorrow was on that particular
today,
blaring our speakers
with anthems of something
or someone
while snorting lines of conversation

off the steering wheel.
Miles of highways,
and roads,
and airwaves—
together—tapping our fingers
and feet to the
beat, and
singing songs we half-way remembered.
From Long Beach
to Long Island,
to somewhere south of Portland,
back east to Poughkeepsie—
isolated delirium convincing our
rhythmic stomping
wherever it was raining.

4.2.15

Not a day goes by
when I don't think about you—
wish that you are well.

10.22.14

I'm mesmerized by
the way that your lips move
around the words that you speak,
and
I'm sorry to interrupt,
but
if I wait another second to kiss you,
I'll crumble.

2.7.14

You
    are
        worthy.
You
    are
        capable.
You
    are
        you.

1.3.14

As you dance in the gardens
across the way,
I think to myself
how I hope that the flowers
will tell you how much
I miss you.

12.15.13

If I could be anything,
I would be the rain
that drips from your lips
as we stand under the stars,
and I would be the pressure
applied at our hips when we kiss;
our every worry falls
so far from our hearts.

Walls and Windows
5.9.16

If I close my eyes, I can almost go there...

Arriving at your home, headlights shining
on a street called Gold Rush— fitting
because it was as if
I struck it rich when I met you.
Climbing the weathered
wood stairs to greet you, I would see you,
peering through the window, eager
and glowing from the slight
suggestion of your smile.
We would go and ascend
to tops of quiet mountains
where we would swim together through
gradients of blue—
fingers interlaced—catching stars
in our mouths like snowflakes,
and falling in love along the way
the way young people do...

I drove past that home the other day
— the one you used to live in—
and wondered if its walls,
and the windows you looked through
feel the way I do with you
gone.

Tranquil
8.25.15

Find me not in gentle voices
or raspy voices,
ambience, convers-
ation,
or rhythm, or rhyme,
or cadence. No,
feel me,
hear me in the silent margins
of moments, in the spaces amongst
words— the tense
pauses,
in the notes that never happened
between notes that did.
Find me, quiet as the mountains—listen
for although I sound of
stillness, I
speak.
I whisper,
"I am ever present,
seek."

1.21.15

The most amazing thing
About her eyes
Was that she always saw
The best in me.

Sometime in 1997

My blue mother
is water in a vase. She smiles.
I smile back and sleep.

10.19.14

I'm just watching
these
autumn leaves
fall from trees
as they do—
softly—
like the way I
fell
for you.

she and i
1.22.15

we sat on the rocks of the shoreline
and touched our toes to the lake below:
she,
in her
yellow sundress,
which danced softly
and rhythmically
through my imagination ever since,
and i,
lost in a reflection where that
yellow sundress
danced gently with the ripples of the
crystal blue water—
longing for her to twirl her toes
and bring end to an
eternal rumination. I've never seen such a
clear summer day—july—not a cloud in the
sky, and
ever since that day—july—her capti-
vating blue eyes reminded me of water.
she was there on a peninsula in long island,
i was eleven. i stood at the shore of the atlantic
staring at my reflection. her dress
danced amongst the waves in the deep blue ocean—
Moonlit
yellow into the horizon.
she was there in denver,
whispering almost Inaudibly in my ear
as they rolled me on a yellow table
to a room where they would dig a mass from
my blue mind.
she said it was only a monkey,
and to this day, i'm unsure what she meant by that,
but i know it gave me comfort.

she was there in a hospital wing in billings
where i've never felt more alone.
she called me on the blue
pay phone,
which hung from the
yellow wall in the hallway,
and told me about a man who had Stolen her heart in
washington.
she laid next to me there as i slept for days,
all the while, giving me comfort.
i woke to see her eyes in the
dark night Skies,
and i traveled in my mind, out the window.
she was there,
and she danced in her sundress.
she was there in the churchyard
where they stored my grandfather's urn—
i was five.
i ran in the yard and played tag with the Yellow
butterflies;
i asked my blue mother
why the only part of my grandfather's body that was
buried
was his lashes;
she was there in the Orchards
dripping in water
when i thought i heard him speak to me
and tell me
hewantedmewithhim.
i was ten.
she stood next to me then in her
yellow sundress,
and held my hand,
providing an Uplifting and calming voice
amongst an angry chorus of screams.
she is with me in my dreams,
and i am without her
so it seems.

3.14.16

I've been missing you
through far too many moments.
Now, come back to me.

7.24.15

A perfect world
would contain every
last thing
that it does today,
save the space
between our bodies.

Kevin A. Murphy

1.25.15

You are
the
ocean
and I
am
lost at sea.

7.21.14

Hold strong to these hands,
for these hands are an anchor
weighting for your love.

7.21.15

What if we
measured success
by the amount
to which
we love ourselves
and others?
What if we
allowed ourselves
fulfillment?

5.15.15

We could spend
every moment for
the rest of our lives
together
and I would still
want more of you—
my sweetest vice,
my softest addiction.

1.24.14

You have a way
of making your way
into my dreams.
Do you intend to?
Or do you stumble there,
unaware, as I unravel
at the seams?

Skipping and Ripples
11.18.13

I am a single stone
upon infinite stones.
I am stationary and quiet.
I am shaped by the waters of this world,
and I'll only move if you move me.
The cracks on my surface
remind you of something in your past,
but you weren't the first to have picked me up,
and you certainly won't be the last.

10.20.15

She is rhythm; she
composes songs
just by being. The ways
that her hips and her lips
move
leave me to wonder
why anyone
ever needed music.

Crave
7.19.15

Eyes closed, I only listen.
It's that time of night when musings spin like cyc

lo
n
e
s

through our minds.
It's that time of night
when young hearts roam free through empty
s p a c e s
in the streets of small towns—summer,
salty air to breathe—and d

o
w
n

alleyways where alley-cats sing to the tune
of a can being kicked.
Whistling, turf-toed, and red-eyed
fucker hasn't sleptindays—but listen—
he has something to say; you might say he has a vision.
It's that time of night,
and there's something to be seen

here,

to be taken from this

here

in the darkness of the black and blue,
bruised like a shiner, midnight hour.
If I
listen to the sounds,
to the
howls,
I hear voices that
crave
for the light.

3.22.16

The bags beneath these
bloodshot eyes
hold the shallow breaths
of one thousand
sleepless nights
spent deep inside my
fractured mind
recalling
countless rested mornings
at your
peaceful side.

3.31.16

Into my arms, love,
against the pulse in my chest—
fall and I'll catch you.

Kevin A. Murphy

Now and Forever
1.29.16

What if we met on the rooftop,
and spoke of right now as if it were
something tangible, until our words faded
into dawn with the constellations? Would
you rest your head on my chest, and gaze
at the stars in amazement, as if they would
always keep burning? As if our souls would
always
keep burning with wonder?
Or would you sit with crossed legs
and half-a-smile, as I wandered miles
and miles into your eyes, all the while
dancing
to the rhythm and the sound of your
voice?
Would you laugh if I told you
there was nowhere else I'd rather be?
As if somehow right now
were a tangible thing? As if we had
a choice to stop time and admire
the silence? Would you reach out your hands
with mine, and grasp the rising sun
or shooting stars: Polaroids of the breaths
from seconds otherwise lost in memory?
If I could give you no logic or reason,
would you join me on the rooftop,
and write now into the open pages
of forever?

5.1.15

I want to spend a
lifetime
convincing you
that you are wrong
about every little thing
you believe is
imperfect
about you.

2.19.15

Set it all to flame;
you can't dry these eyes;
I've been staring at the sun
my entire life.

11.21.13

You caught my eye
like a snowflake
reflecting moonlight
as I walked by.

11.29.14

I suppose what is most
difficult today
is becoming the man
we both knew I could be,
and knowing
you'll never meet him.

8.29.16

There are moments left
that would be only half-lived
if spent without you.

Broken Haiku
10.20.15

What of growing old?
There are these days, and
I've been
   spending them
      alone.

Blanket
6.17.15

The better part of three years
spent searching, attempting to find
what I was made of,
when the only thing I needed,
was to rest in your presence
for one moment,
for once.

My heart beats to the rhythm
you dance to;
it pounds so fast sometimes,
and you are all
that makes it calm.

I wrapped myself around you,
because I needed something
to hold on to
when it became clear
that I was created from a cloth,
which carries an insatiable need
to unravel.

If falling apart is inevitable,
then maybe my heart
would beat a little slower,
and perhaps our threads
would become entangled,
allowing you to
hold me
together,
if I were to lay here
with you
in this moment—
warm.

Kevin A. Murphy

Palindrome Poem I
9.18.14

Night
becomes
day.
Awakenings ignite ideas.
Loveliness expresses itself
in everything.
Eyes open wide
unveils beauty.
Today is magnificent—
Live!
Magnificent is today—
beauty unveils
wide open eyes.
Everything in
itself expresses loveliness.
Ideas ignite awakenings.
Day
becomes
night.

Moloch
9.28.16

I am the nine-times-forgotten and seven-
times-forgiven son of ominous sun-
sets setting over the peak of Makalu.
I am the outstretched arms of archangels
whose fingers never touched the skin
of glistening, succulent, ripe, red apples
before they fell to ground. I am the cracks
beneath the feet of the suits and white collars
who march emphatically through Times
Square, across the Brooklyn Bridge to
Flatbush Avenue, wearing ribbons pinned
to the lapel, and holding signs that call on
God to save us,
and of those who
don't own collars, but wear
tattered blue jeans, yellow helmets, white helmets,
and orange vests—who carry hammers,
jackhammers, and screwdrivers,
spending their entire lives hammering, screwing,
and getting screwed—marching tentatively through
Times
Square, across the Brooklyn Bridge to
Flatbush Avenue, holding signs that call on
God to save the U.S.. I am the broken pavement
beneath the pacing;
I am not the stars in the sky, or the words
in these lines, but you can find me in the
spacing.

You can feel me in the twisting limbs of willows,
alongside dirt pathways, and through the endless fog
of morning. You can see me in the distant bloodshot
gaze of academics—whose eyes remain wide open
into the crack of fucking dawn—writing pages,

55

and pages of answers, still coming up with questions,
and never, ever, fucking. You can hear me in the echoes
of the most southeastern corner of a schoolyard,
where children chatter, and run with strawberries
on their knees, making games of sticks and stones,
and walking slowly—balancing along a splintered beam—
where only yards away, grown men also play games,
on a short par three, drinking whiskey, and making
jokes about marriage; I am the laughter and the silence
thereafter. You can smell me in the kitchens of lonely
housewives who cook and cook, and clean, and wake
each day to do the same, wearing incomprehensible
amounts of makeup to cover their wrinkling faces,
and also every morning ironing wrinkles from their
husbands' collars, and in the haze hovering over L.A.,
splendidly masking the pigmentation of the sunset,
with the by-products of every serotonin-deficient soul—
living and dead—from Pomona to Westlake Village.
You can taste me on your tongue if you are mindful
when you breathe; I am the lies
that go between your teeth.

6.14.14

The way the waves
roll against each other
in perfect harmony
reminds me of the way
our bodies would touch
as we would turn
within our sheets,
and looking out
at the ocean beneath me,
I realize
my reminiscence
spans only as far
as the sea.

11.9.15

She's loved by many
because she has the softest
characteristics.

5.29.15

I don't drink
whiskey
anymore;
I drink dreams,
and I'm
always
thirsty.

1.19.15

Somewhere deep in
the mountains,
and under the stars,
we spoke,
and laughed,
and sang for hours.
We lay beside the constant
flow of the river,
where for the first
and only time,
I held you.

5.30.15

Forgive me for being so quiet;
I lost my breath
when you walked in
and spoke—
your lips,
so violet,
and my tongue,
like someone tied it.

12.24.14

When day turns to night,
my feet will find their way with
your love as my light.

Sister
6.13.15

I need you to
promise me
that if you
find yourself
surrounded by darkness,
you will use your
hands
as eyes
until you find your way;
I need you to
reach out your hands
because mine
will be always reaching back,
and I will be damned
if I don't
pull you
to safety.

6.26.16

Her eyes change colors
like the evening sky, and I
love chasing sunsets.

4.30.15

You are the music I live with;
I have heard your voice
in every note
of every song
that has ever met my ears.

12.31.14

All of these love notes,
and not one as poetic
as the thought of you.

Sinkhole
11.23.13

It's funny how fast this town dies down,
as if it were suddenly sucked into the ground around it.
A select few stand confused, lonely,
astounded,
bound to the addictions by which they're
tied down,
unsure of the direction that
leads them,
unscathed by the destiny that will inevitably
greet them—
the cold hand that will eventually
beat them—to the ground beneath them.
Their feet silently pound to the beat,
and the violent sound of the weak,
as they drown their souls with a drink,
that they think
will release them,
and as the liquor would do
if they were to
pour the bottle out,
they spiral down the sink
that defeats them.

Kevin A. Murphy

Emeralds
(Crossing Signs)
10.14.14

I swear she has emeralds
in her emerald
green
eyes,
and light was created solely
for the purpose
of shining on her hair.
Trees have been living
for hundreds of years,
wishing
the entire time,
that sometime,
she would use them for shade.
She could walk into a ball
wearing sweatpants,
and
steal the attention
of
the entire room.
She could walk into any wedding,
and steal the eyes of the groom.
I swear she has emeralds
in her emerald
green eyes.
I once made her a necklace
for around ten dollars
out of beads,
and when she reached behind her neck
to fasten that necklace
with the gentle
-touch-
of the tips of her fingers,

the beads became diamonds,
and
don't ask me how she did this,
unless you believe in angels.
When she fastened that necklace
between the gentle
-touch-
of her lips,
I envied that necklace more
than anything I had ever envied
before.
Even though I have this messy habit
of staring at the ground,
I found my eyes staring
at her gentle, emerald
green
eyes,
and I swear that
somehow
she soothed me;
I swear to the heavens,
she moved me.
She thought out loud
with me, and said that
maybe some day
we'd meet again under
(crossing)street(signs),
and
she'd be unable to help
but approach me.
She imagined we'd speak again
as we always had, and I think it some sort
of romantic tragedy that
that was the night before
she left.
She's been gone for some years now,
and I
hope like hell

she's happy wherever it is that she is.
I thought I saw her standing
under
(crossing)street(signs)
one night:
emeralds and
diamonds,
sweatpants,
gentle fingertips,
and the gentle
-touch-
of her lips,
but
she never approached me,
and
I've been standing here
under (crossing)street(signs)
ever since.

Fireworks for You
7.4.14

I gaze into the night
as far as my vision will allow.
I wish upon a star,
and as I send my dreams afar,
I pray that you're watching too,
as the star explodes
into the darkness—
a million different colors
for you.

3.29.14

As tenebrous silhouettes of days past
disintegrate from above his shoulders,
a radiant hue emerges along the horizon,
where for the first time,
the sun intersects with the earth.

The contours of pine trees—
upstanding and unwavering—
suggest rebirth.

2.21.15

They say
no one's perfect,
but I say that's a lie—
I hold the living proof
in my arms
every night.

Kevin A. Murphy

Palindrome Poem II
4.3.15

Sounds
soothing,
voices soft
with
gentle whispers
and blue
water colors
her
-love-
her
colors water
blue and
whispers gentle
with
soft voices,
soothing
sounds.

9.26.16

I don't know
     if I ever
          told you but
   when I
     hold you, I am
          whole. All else is
     glitter.

12.19.15

I want to be the T-shirt
you sleep in.
Not the necklace you wear,
with careful curls of hair, which move
with you,
like wind through trees.
Or the ring that lives on your delicate
finger, where I could surely
linger in your touch, and exist
to make you blush with a complimenting
shimmer. I could be close to you
there—resting tender on your skin, and
worn with pride and placid beauty—
but I want to be the T-shirt you wear
with stars shooting through the darkness,
moon beam-
ing on your body like white light
on gardens of irises; I want to be
the fabric you sleep in.
Feel my kisses
while you're dreaming,
pull me closer
with your breathing.

Similarly
9.19.15

There's the thought of
dangerous beauty,
and similarly,
there's you.

There are slowly floating
clouds in skies of blue,
and similarly,
there's the way that you move.

There's the way you
approach things
like you have something to prove,
and similarly,
there's the way I
want to
approach you
like I have nothing to lose.

11.1.14

I had been trying to forget you
for forever, telling myself
that I don't even know
who you are
anymore,
but I think I moved on
when I realized
that you're the same person
you've always been.

8.23.14

You smile in my dreams;
I'm weak in the knees; you're so
irresistible.

4.4.16

I've seen this before:
you walk away with my heart,
and I stay quiet.

Find Happiness in Right Now
8.19.14

Long hair
and unkempt beards,
tight shirts
and a mangled
self-image, and
self-destruction lurking around
every river bend bending around
and around,
and all the mountain's tops abound.
Showers with hands,
sinks and water,
and a Wal-Mart bathroom,
and possibly something to eat.
A cigarette and fifteen more
cigarettes. A van
with wheels
and bongs;
I put my lighter in my mouth
and tried to light it with my pipe.
And friends.
Friends!
And laughing.
Pizza in little parlors,
California basement rock shows.
We met my sister in a coffee shop
in Coeur d'Alene for her birthday.
Fields outside that
somehow smelled only like marijuana
from inside a van that smelled only like
marijuana. Endless marijuana,
and two 40-ounces each and every night.
An infatuation with the idea that
one might be
able to be

inloveandaloneforever.
Singing songs with beauti-
ful harmonies: full harmonies.
Thinking, "this might be the
single situation I could
find happiness in right now."
Wondering of the effect
a brain tumor might have on one's heart,
wandering through fields of emptiness and nostalgia
in a place I'd never been before, attempting to
find happiness in right now.
You never answered the phone.
The pavement under the bridge
called my name that night. That night,
I walked around for hours
in a frenzy of unknowingness,
loneliness, and adrenaline—
wanting to write,
but not being able to
write,
and wanting to talk to you,
but not being able to talk
to you,
and wondering if I knew any words
that I had never written with a pen.
The only thing that kept me alive
that night
was my brothers, sleeping
in my conscience. Consciousness
some 50 yards away.
A different city every day,
and faces and people,
and liquor chased with hundred-foot-tall
Redwoods, Northern California,
coastal contemplations seeking
meanings and dissecting the beauty of
waves. The vastness of an ocean curling,
riptide ripping myself to pieces

over what? And here I was having the time of my life,
running ramped, kelly green
moss-lined rock faces, trails
leading directly into déjà vu.
I found something there.
I found YOU there.
I found at least one nickel on the ground in front of a
doorway
leading to 1,825 lost days and I lost
myself there.
In white-capped snow-peaks: Sacramento,
and
rolling hills:
San Jose with muffin tops,
the steep streets of San Francisco
selling something my parents purchased
in the sixties,
I lost myself there.
From Haight street to fourth of july pass,
to future fourth of july's, and
Hated fourth of july's from the past,

I lost

my

self

there.

2.4.15

She spends her nights dancing
under the light of the moon—
pirouetting
in the silence,
softly twirling on her feet—
and all alone there,
she holds her hands as if
she held the hands
of someone.

Snowflakes
10.2.14

Immaculate snowflakes
rest on your
immaculate silken hair,
and your lips quiver
gently in the cold.

Your smile is flawless
like snowflakes—
unique and exemplary—
it shines through your
trembling lips,
and your engaging eyes,
they encage me alive.

I could gaze at you
for a lifetime,
and I think I'd float
like snowflakes.

I could stare at your
reflection
forever,
and I think I'd float;

I think I'd dance
like snowflakes.

6.1.14

Walking down that sidewalk
covered in mist, I was so sure
of who I would become
and where I was going,
but as I climbed the stairs
leading to your house that night,
my destiny became self-conscious,
and I became lost in your eyes.

6.1.15

I am so
completely
flawed,
and still,
I am
cocooned
by your
perfect love.

9.20.16

You watched me die from
a broken heart. Now, see me
come back from the dead.

Guide Her
4.5.16

America, I speak to you calmly
and in whispers,
for your rage is double-faced
and ever-brewing.
Did you lose your eyes
in the fights ensuing from your temper,
and if not, what made you blind?
America, thank you for being so kind;
the world needs your bombs,
and you know it. America,
you turned red skin to white,
and you are oh so blue,
but you never cry—you
never show it. America,
the price of love is high,
and you are stockpiling lives
to throw against your opponents.
America, I long to pick your roses,
but you are burning on Mount Horeb,
and you haven't built the Western Wall.
America, do you listen at all?
The voices of two hundred years are cooing.
America, fuck your kindness.
America, we love you.

8.14.16

My hands
are unfinished puzzles,
and yours,
the missing pieces.

What would I not give
to be completed?

What will appear if our fingers
touch?

Still, I Write
4.25.16

How fast
it flies; I barely see it pass
by—
all the movements, fluctuations—
time.

The truth is,
it is all set in motion
by this mess in my mind
that I am merely trying to untangle;
introspection dangles from a strand
of knotted twine. Eloquent arrangements
of syllables elude me. Still,
I write. I write
to decelerate my racing
consciousness—an attempt
to extract some sort of
epiphanic thought from this—all of this
spinning.
Nothing more. Nothing
less.

4.13.15

Every time I close my eyes,
I fall asleep for days—
either to escape
or dream about you.

10.9.14

Take my hand and run;
the stars above will guide us.
We can change the world.

10.12.15

Your touch reminds me of
rain-kissed daisies
at early June sunrise, and
your lips taste like the moon—
refreshing,
like sleeping in 'til noon.
You are radiant with
all the colors of a day,
but you loved me in slivers,
so every time I see your face,
or hear your name,
it sends shivers
through my brain.

12.24.15

Let it percolate—
the good in our hearts, the love—
let it spill over.

1.4.16

I could describe this emotion
as standing at the lip of the ocean:
a blue, serene horizon.

I swear I can see forever,
and I innately desire to swim;
I am drawn to the calm of your eyes.

8.16.15

You are the rays of light,
which made their way through
branches and leaves,
and into my scope of vision
by way of luck,
or destiny.
You have my eyes,
and soon, when today turns to
night,
we can rest under
the moon,
and you can have
the rest of me.

12.19.14

I hope that you are well, my friend.
I hope that you can see what is happening,
and I hope that this liquid—
this poisonous liquid—
doesn't kill you.
I feel for you, friend,
because I have been
where you are right now,
and I know how difficult it is
to be in that place,
but I know that you have what it takes;
I know that you can do this.

Of My Love
5.17.15

Forgive me if I evaporate or
disintegrate, upon
the next match being lit,
and forgive me as well,
if my screams bear nothing
but the silent wind in the spaces between
the stars when I leave. Forgive me
if I exist forever in melancholic nooks
between the chaotic galaxies,
and not on Earth or in heaven,
for perhaps I was not meant
for the earth or the heavens,
and perhaps they were not meant for me.
Forgive me.
Forgive me if the birds sing songs
before you've had your coffee,
and if I sing while you are trying to sleep,
for my apologies move steady
with the pale blue wisps of the clouds in the
dark
night
sky,
and in the rising yellow of morning.
Forgive me for mourning.
And forget me. But hold me
when my tears—as raindrops
during soft and warm sunrise,
or the hazy mist of the night—
roll down your cheeks,
and fall to fill the cracks
in the sidewalk
with little currents
of my love.

5.5.15

Had I known
it would be the last time
I would stare into your
incredibly
gentle eyes,
I would have
never
gone
home.

1.28.15

Climb into our bed.
Leave your cares at the door and
your clothes on the floor.

1.13.15

I'm unsure what
forever feels like,
but I'm certain
it would feel
better with you.

7.10.16

I've been chewing gold
and spitting toward the sky
(new stars for wishing).

8.30.16

If you check my pulse,
you'll feel a concerto: an arrangement
in which my heart serves as only a
metronome, but to its cadence, delivers
crescendos and decrescendos, and
crashing waves:
moments
that would make you dance
without mov-
ing a muscle. You'd be swept away in the notes
like sand by sea at sunrise (velvet
skies the color of your
blush),
brilliantly isolated in white light
cast on the stage of a brand new day—
performing your music;
you could find yourself in my-
self,
my veins, the flow and the rhythm of my
heart.
Feel my pulse, for there is a
beat, and you
are playing the solo.

12.3.13

I am an unopened letter
that you slide across a table.
I don't know why I feel this way;
I only know that you move me.

10.30.14

Lend me your soft soul—
I will knead mine into yours,
and we will make love.

4.7.15

I will spend
every waking
moment
placing stones
and building them
into a bridge between
you and I so that
if you should decide
to ever come back
you won't have to fight
the current.

4.7.16

When you tilt your head ever
so slightly, I see a suggestion of your smile
sparkle in the window. In the reflection,
you are reflecting, serene and smooth, as
water wandering whimsically
through relaxed riverbeds;
you are reserved yet resolved. You are
velvet violets in my vision,
and I am distracted,
diverted in a distant daydream,
gallivanting through gardens of your
glances. When you tilt your head ever
so slightly, the reflection in the window
dances.

2.13.15

I know this isn't
drowning
because I've drowned
countless times
before,
so why is it that I lie here
with
flooded lungs
atop the ocean floor?

2.6.15

My love for her
is the water of a leaky faucet,
which stands in a meadow,
dripping,
little by little,
through all of the seasons,
never freezing,
from now
until forever.

Short Stories

Flowers

She counted backward from ten like she learned. She imagined being young again, and being free from her mind. She remembered the way that as a young girl, she'd bundle daffodils together by tying a few blades of grass around their stems. Alone in her backyard, the world was anything she wanted it to be, and it was always beautiful.

Remembering her childhood made her happy because it took her to a less confusing time. Annabelle always loved flowers—there was something about them, which made her calm. She used to say that when she got older, she'd grow endless gardens—beautiful gardens containing every conceivable color. She imagined she'd spend her days digging in the soil, giving her gardens the gentle care they required.

Annabelle learned everything she knew about flowers from her mother during the bright summer days of her backyard childhood. She learned that seeds need love, and that when they aren't given love, they grow to be wilted, lifeless flowers, which aren't beautiful at all. She wanted to be beautiful, and she wanted her flowers to be beautiful as well.

* * * *

Annabelle sat hunching with her back against a wall in the hallway leading to her bedroom. She held her head in the unsteadiness of her grey, trembling hands, which held a bouquet of wilting daffodils tied together by a few blades of grass at the stems. She breathed deeply, attempting to recollect the previous moments. She counted backward from ten, confused. Her daffodils broke from the few blades of grass they'd been tied together with—scattering across the floor as she reached her hands toward her face. She felt open wounds with the shaking tips of her fingers. Riverbeds of blood on her cheeks began to dry and made the skin of her face itch and feel taught. A swell of pressure pulsed behind her left eye—the fluorescent hallway blinded—it seemed that Lily had beaten her again.

* * * *

"Anna. Anna, sweetie, wake up." A soft voice woke Annabelle from a slumber, "My name is Dr. Dahlia. I'm helping take care of you here at Saint Alyssum Hospital. We've met before. Do you remember me?"

"I...I'm not sure," Annabelle responded in a soft, quivering voice.

"I need to talk to you about last night, is that okay?"

Annabelle didn't respond at first as she became lost for a moment, gazing past the hospital walls to a field full of flowers.

"Annabelle?"

"Oh...yes. Yes, I'm sorry. That's fine."

"Anna, why are you here? What happened last night? Can you tell me how you got these cuts on your face?"

Annabelle counted backward from ten like she learned, "I...I was attacked by Lily. She's done this before. She claws at me and scratches my face. I can't ever seem to stop her. One second I'm alone with my flowers, and the next...well...I don't know how to explain it."

"Go on, Anna. You're doing great; I'm listening."

"The next thing I know, my face is bleeding, and I can feel the cuts with my fingers. I never see her, but I know it's her. She's done this since I was little, Lily hates me."

"Did you look at your cuts in the mirror, Anna?"

Tears began to swell in Anna's eyes as she spoke, "I don't like looking in the mirror anymore; I know I'm not beautiful. I don't feel ok...I don't think I'll ever feel ok."

The doctor watched Anna begin to drift off as if into

a dream. Annabelle's head fell to her shoulder, as her body could no longer carry the burden of supporting its weight. Annabelle slouched almost lifeless in her chair, except for that she breathed short, struggling breaths.

Dr. Dahlia kneeled in front of Annabelle, holding her cold hands, "Anna, sweetie. Oh Anna, come back."

Annabelle blinked her teary eyes a few times before regaining consciousness and looking back at the gentle doctor, "What's wrong with me?"

"Anna, sweetheart, I'm so sorry. You have to think hard. You know this; you've learned this. Annabelle, sweetie, Lily didn't hurt you. Lily is your mother, she passed away when you were nine."

* * * *

Annabelle felt herself drifting. She opened her eyes to find herself sitting in a garden full of daffodils dahlias, alyssums, and lilies. Anna had always loved flowers—there was something about them, which made

her calm.

Long Island, Childhood, and Bike Rides

We used to go to a little beach town on Long Island, New York for vacations when I was growing up; it was where my dad spent his childhood. The town was surrounded on three sides by the Atlantic, and on the fourth side, a four-way street led to the typical things one might imagine when thinking of New York: the lights and the sounds of the Big Apple.

I much preferred the sights and sounds of the small beach town we stayed in. Perhaps the rolling tide was more reminiscent of the setting I came from: the unaltered forests of Montana.

I spent much of those summer vacations walking barefoot with my sister and cousins—four blocks to the public beach and four blocks back to the house my dad was raised in. We'd spend entire days on that beach—swimming, burning our skin, and eating ice cream—

much like our parents probably did some decades ago.

In fact, I remember wondering how those exact

experiences might have affected my father had he

experienced them the way we did, and how they might

affect me.

* * * *

Some nights, I'd ride the ten-speed I found in the

shed of my father's childhood home around the 16-block

perimeter of that peninsula town, listening to the

resonation of the crashing tide. My sister and cousins

would stay at the house laughing and getting into

trouble while our parents became increasingly

intoxicated, and as night increasingly encroached on

morning. Those joyrides were therapeutic for me: a

chance to escape and to think. At fourteen years old, I

had just been diagnosed with depression and was still

getting used to having bottles of pills on my nightstand.

The doctors would find a tumor on the left-frontal lobe of

my brain the following summer, which I've often

thought went a long way in explaining those midnight bike rides I spent alone and lost in thought. My sister and cousins didn't take pills; my sister and cousins stayed and goofed around in the house where our parents were getting drunk. Yet I was out in the twilight, churning my legs with my feet on pedals—so fast that the chain would sometimes break free of the gears it was fastened to. I wanted to break free as well. There was something healing about the saline wind in my hair, and the openness of the ocean, which allowed myself and my thoughts to wander wherever they pleased.

I Don't Feel Hungry

I'm writing this to whomever might stumble upon my notebook because I'm not sure what's real anymore, and if what I'm thinking is true, I need to tell my story. It's a rainy night in Bellevue, Washington and I'm looking out the window of my parent's spare bedroom at the tire-swing I used to spend hours reading in as a child. At least I think that's where I am...I'll get to that soon, but I suppose I should tell you who I am first. My name is Amy Pierson. I'm 27 years old, single, and I worked in marketing until around 6 months ago. I have...I had a twin sister named Beth, which I suppose is where my story starts.

Beth and I were both diagnosed with a rare genetic disorder called Wilson's disease around the same time last year. The disease causes copper to build up in a person's organs, which can lead to organ failure and eventually death. Doctors put Beth and me on treatment plans as soon as we were diagnosed, but as the treatment went on, and days began to go by, the two of us only got worse. Grasping for anything that might get their daughters healthy again, our parents sought out the help of Dr. Linda Hazzard, who runs an experimental medical clinic a couple hours north of Bellevue on Whidbey Island. Dr. Hazzard's methods aim to treat disease by starving the patients of all food save broth, water, and the occasional orange. I realize how ridiculous it probably sounds for someone to take their daughters to a clinic, which starves its patients in hopes that they get better, but I think my parents were desperate, and the clinic boasted that its alternative treatments could be the cure to our disease. In fact, within a month of beginning our treatment with Dr. Hazzard, both Beth and I began to feel relief from the pain we'd been experiencing. I remember sitting down with Beth to write letters to our parents (there were no phones for patients in the hospital wing), and telling them how much better we were feeling, but the relief

was short-lived for both of us.

I began to notice as I looked around the hospital

wing that the patients seemed to be unusually weak and

extremely disoriented, even crazy. In retrospect, I

should have seen that the starvation was slowly killing

all of us, but we believed we were getting better. Dr.

Hazzard would talk to each of us daily at supper, which

consisted of a small bowl of broth and a glass of water,

and was surprisingly fulfilling; it's funny how small

your appetite becomes when you've eaten nearly

nothing for weeks. The doctor would talk to us at

dinner, telling us that the disorientation we experienced

was a side effect of the treatment, and that it would go

away when we recovered and could eat full meals again.

I think that we believed her because she was so kind

and genuine, and because she worked so hard with each

of us. However, I eventually began to sense that

something wasn't right at the hospital.

One evening, as the patients were wandering the hospital wing floor and gazing out the windows, another patient—a young lady with wiry blonde hair and distant blue eyes named Emelia—told me that Dr. Hazzard was starving us in order to purify our blood. Emelia often told elaborate, extravagant stories, so I wasn't sure what to make of this. She said that the doctor was eventually going to kill us and bathe herself in our blood because she believed it gave her youth. I remember thinking that Emelia was either feeling delusional from the treatment or telling another one of her stories, but as I looked around, I noticed that all of the patients were women no older than 30.

A few weeks later, I awoke in the middle of the night to the sound of blood-curdling screams, which I knew to be coming from my sister. Naturally, I jumped out of bed to help her, but realized as soon as I touched the doorknob that I was locked in. I was so weak, and the thought occurred that I was only dreaming, or that I was just experiencing a delusion as a side effect from the treatment, so I lay back down to sleep. The next morning Beth didn't show up for our breakfast orange and glass of water with the rest of the patients. Dr. Hazzard told me that Beth had been sent home the night before with my parents because she was doing so well with her disease. Call it premonition, or sisterly instinct, or whatever you want, I knew my sister was dead.

That day, I wrote a letter to my parents telling them all about Dr. Hazzard and the hospital. I asked them to come get me before both Beth and I were dead, but I wondered if any of the letters I wrote from the hospital ever made it to my parents' mailbox anyway. As the doctor was making her way around the cafeteria to talk to each of the patients at dinner that night, I asked to be excused to use the restroom down the hall. I was surprised that Dr. Hazzard let me away by myself given the prior night's happenings, but I suppose I hadn't let her know that I knew my sister was dead. Regardless, I decided this was my chance to break out of the hospital. I snuck into Dr. Hazzard's office, broke out her window, jumped to the ground, and began to sprint. I don't know how I had the energy to run anywhere, except for that I was running for my life.

I must have been running for five minutes straight when I came to a small building with a tire-swing in front of it and light shining through its only window. I crept up as quietly as I could to look inside. Before my mind was able to register the sight of the blood-filled bath and corner full of rotting bodies, I felt a pair of arms wrap around me from behind. I screamed as loud as I could as Dr. Hazzard carried me back towards the hospital, but I had little faith that anyone would save me from my death that night.

As we approached the hospital, my parents came running from the parking lot. My father, a former college football player, speared Dr. Hazzard and myself to the ground before laying an elbow into the doctor's face. Dr. Hazzard was unconscious and my parents carried me to their car. They told me they had driven up to visit my sister and me after work that night and heard my screams when they got out of their car. I cried in my mother's arms as I told her everything about the hospital—Beth's murder included—and I fell asleep to the sound of my father's voice on the phone with the police.

It's been three days since arriving here—the home that I grew up in. My parents tell me that Dr. Hazzard has been arrested and that I'm safe now. Yet as I look out the window at the tire swing, I wonder if what I see is real. I realize that all of this might only be a delusion. I might be at the hospital still, even though I don't feel hungry.

ABOUT THE AUTHOR

Kevin A. Murphy is a student at Carroll College in Helena, MT, where he studies psychology. After obtaining his undergraduate degree, he hopes to attend graduate school in order to pursue a career in either mental health counseling or sports psychology.

Murphy began writing poetry at age 9 when an artist in residence visited his fourth grade classroom. Kevin continued writing sporadically through his teenage years, and through a time in which he underwent brain surgery and continually struggled with depression.

The ability to express himself creatively through words seemed to have slipped through Murphy's hands when he began drinking heavily in his early twenties.

Kevin gave up drinking after a five year period of alcoholism and began to feel his creativity coming back. A short time into his sobriety, Murphy began writing *Words Versus Meanings*.

When not writing, Kevin competes for the Carroll College golf team, snowboards the Rocky Mountains, draws in his sketchbook, and enjoys time with his family and friends.

www.ingramcontent.com/pod-product-compliance
Lightning Source LLC
Chambersburg PA
CBHW020504030426
42337CB00011B/224